HORRIBLE HISTORIES

GRUESOME GUIDES

STRATFORD
UPON-AVON

TERRY DEARY

ILLUSTRATED BY
MIKE PHILLIPS

SCHOLASTIC

For David and the ghosts at the Shrieve's House
on Sheep Street. TD

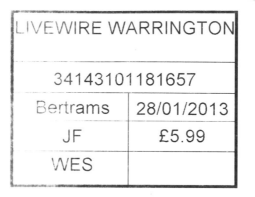

A division of Scholastic Ltd
London ~ New York ~ Toronto ~ Sydney ~ Auckland
Mexico City ~ New Delhi ~ Hong Kong

First published in the UK by Scholastic Ltd, 2006
This edition published 2010

Text © Terry Deary, 2006
Illustrations © Mike Phillips, 2006
Cover illustration © Martin Brown, 2006

978 1407 11078 3

Page layout services provided by Quadrum Solutions Ltd, Mumbai, India
Printed and bound by CPI Group (UK) Ltd, Croydon, CR0 4YY

4 6 8 10 9 7 5

The right of Terry Deary, Mike Phillips and Martin Brown to be identified as
the author and illustrators of this work respectively has been asserted by
them in accordance with the Copyright, Designs and Patents Act, 1988.

CONTENTS

Introduction

Stratford.

Its full name is Stratford-upon-Avon because it is built on the banks of the river Avon, not on the river.

This cute little town is famous for one thing: the writer William Shakespeare was born there. He went off to London to be famous but he returned to Stratford to die...

Nowadays Stratford is pretty and quiet, but when Will lived here it wasn't so quaint. The truth is life in those days was grim. One person in three lived in poverty. If the poverty didn't get you then dirty water might. If you survived street fights then you might not survive bites from the fleas that carried the plague.

If you go to Stratford today you'll see the way it NEVER was in Tudor times. You'll see a bit of a fib.

What you need is a book that tells you the terrible truth of what REALLY went on in Stratford's grubby and violent past.

You need a horrible history of Stratford.

Well, dear reader, as it happens you have one in your sweaty little hand. You've opened it now. So I hope you've paid for it!

If you have, then read on...

Stratford timeline

55 BC–AD 200 The Romans come, they see, they conquer. They also give the place a name – they call it Street-ford ... and a 'ford' is a place where you can cross a river. The river is the Avon so the place becomes Street-ford upon Avon.

691 There is a Saxon monastery in Stratford (around where Holy Trinity Church is today). By the time the Normans arrive in 1066 it has gone, but the old town is built around the church that is left.

1086 The Normans come to count the Stratford homes for King William's 'Domesday Book'. There are just 29 houses, but lots of sheep.

1196 The Forest of Arden, next to Stratford, is being cleared. Richard I allows a new market to be built and a new town springs up. The New Stratford people have to worship in the Old Stratford church. They are not happy. Old and new don't get on. The town is now up to 40 houses.

1490 Rich Sir Hugh Clopton pays to have a bridge built over the Avon. No need to ford the river now. Maybe they should change the name to Strat-bridge. They don't.

1564 The plague comes to Stratford and kills many. But baby Will Shakespeare, born on 23 April, survives...

1616 ...Then, on 23 April 1616, Shakespeare dies.

1643 In the English Civil War the Roundheads take Stratford. They store their gunpowder in the Market Hall ... until it explodes. They also damage Clopton Bridge.

1645 That purple-spotted plague is back to make Stratford suffer again. And the rats die in their thousands too. Ahhhh!

1760s People start to get interested in Shakespeare and Stratford becomes a centre for tourists. Stratford starts to get interested in making money from tourists.

1892 A famous painting of Shakespeare is discovered by Sir Desmond Flower and loaned to the Royal Shakespeare Theatre Company. So THAT'S what Shakespeare looked like! Er, no. We now know it's a fake, painted around 1830.

2001 The people of Stratford are upset. Tourist buses are going round the town non-stop and passengers are peering in their windows. The locals win and there are fewer buses.

Medieval mayhem

In the Middle Ages, Stratford was a quiet little village, but nearby there were bloody battles and beheadings...

Simon de Montfort (1208–65), Earl of Leicester

Simon was a rebel baron. He told King Henry III...

YOU'RE SPENDING TOO MUCH MONEY ON FOREIGN WARS!

BUT I'M THE KING! THAT'S WHAT KINGS DO!

De Montfort took the King and Prince Edward prisoner. But in 1265 Edward escaped and raised an army.

De Montfort decided to meet up with his son at Warwick, near Stratford, but Prince Ed got there first. He smashed the army of Simon's son. (They were asleep in tents outside the castle at the time – which was a dozy thing to do.)

Then Prince Edward caught up with de Montfort's army at Evesham. He picked his twelve strongest knights and told them...

YOU ARE OUR DEATH SQUAD. YOUR JOB IS TO KILL DE MONTFORT IN BATTLE!

De Montfort's army was trapped in a loop of the river. His Welsh soldiers charged up the hill screaming a war cry – they were battered by Prince Edward's army and ran back down the hill screaming, 'Help! I want to go home to Wales.'

The Welsh ran away.

Simon told his men…

Let us offer our souls to God because our bodies belong to the enemy.

They prayed. They charged. They were massacred. Even those Welsh soldiers were chopped down as they tried to run away.

De Montfort was killed with a lance in the throat. His body was hacked to pieces and bits of arms and legs sent all around the country. His body was buried at Evesham Abbey.

But his head was sent to Lady Mortimer, the wife of his killer.

THANKS, JUST WHAT I ALWAYS WANTED!

GURGLE!

Prince Ed, the Evesham winner, went on to be King Edward I and that's when he joined up with Guy de Beauchamp, tenth earl of Warwick (1278–1315).

Bloody Blacklow Hill

Good guy Guy de Beauchamp was a great soldier for King Edward I and a help in defeating the savage Scots. King Edward said…

And then Edward I died. Guy was there at the King's side. Loyal to the end.

But then he turned into bad-guy Guy. He did NOT like Ed's son, the new king, Edward II. And he really, REALLY hated the new King's mate, Piers Gaveston.

Gaveston called Guy 'The Black Dog of Arden'.

Gaveston ruled the country while Edward went off to France to get married and he upset just about all of the English lords by lording it over them. They went to war and captured Gaveston. Guy took a savage revenge on him.

Gaveston was dragged from his prison in Dedington Castle and taken down to a group of armed men. Their leader said…

Gaveston was made to walk barefoot to Warwick Castle. It was nearly 30 miles.

Guy gave Gaveston a joke fanfare of trumpets – played very badly.

Then Guy and the Earl of Lancaster gave Gaveston a quick trial. You know the sort of thing…

YOU'RE CHARGED WITH TREASON, HOW DO YOU PLEAD? GUILTY? THOUGHT SO. I SENTENCE YOU TO DEATH. OFF WITH HIS HEAD!

ER…

Gaveston grovelled to Lancaster but it did him no good. He was taken out to the banks of the river Avon and his head was struck off and his blood spilled into the dust.[1]

NO MORE MR NICE GUY

I JUST KNEW HE WAS GOING TO SAY THAT

There is a horribly historical story that may just be true. Four shoemakers took the corpse of Piers Gaveston and presented it to Guy. He was not amused.

1 A book written at the time shows Guy of Warwick standing over the headless body of Gaveston. But the *Horrible Histories* TRUTH is Gaveston was executed on lands that belonged to the Earl of Lancaster. It was Lancaster who was in charge of the execution … even if Guy set it up.

A stone found at Blacklow Hill in Leek Wootton, ten miles from Stratford, marks the bloodstained spot. It says…

Stratford legends and lies

Everyone knows Shakespeare was a local lad but some people like to believe that Stratford was the home of TWO other English legends.

The truth about Georgie

In 1349 St Edward was sacked!

He had been 'Patron Saint' of England for 300 years but now King Edward III said he wanted St George instead.

MOST people will tell you that St George was born in Palestine. But *Horrible Histories* can tell you the amazing truth – a 1500s writer called Richard Johnson said that St George was born at Caludon Castle near Stratford.

Johnson said…

> *George was the son of Lord Albert. He wore a blood red cross on his arm and a dragon on his chest.*

Now you will be able to tell your friends one amazing fact…

ST GEORGE WAS SAID TO BE A FAMOUS SON OF WARWICKSHIRE AND ST GEORGE'S DAY IS 23 APRIL

SO?

Of course Shakespeare also DIED on 23 April … his fifty-second birthday. It must have really spoiled the party…

The real rotten Robin

Robin Hood is also known as Robin of Loxley. Many writers have said…

Ah, but there is a little village called Loxley in Warwickshire, just five miles from Stratford. What if he came from there?

In the days of Richard the Lionheart the land was owned by Robin Fitz Odo of Loxley. This Robin rebelled against the King and lost his lands. He would then have been an outlaw.

There is a gravestone in Loxley churchyard that looks just like an old drawing of Robin Hood's gravestone.

Robin Hood is now famous for robbing the rich to pay the poor. But the old stories don't say that. They say he was a cruel warrior. One of the oldest Robin Hood poems tells a story of rotten Robin the ruthless.

ROBIN'S GREAT ENEMY WAS GUY OF GISBORNE

I AM CLEVER ENOUGH TO CATCH ROBIN OF LOXLEY

SO HE THINKS HE'S A WISE GUY

HE WENT INTO THE FOREST TO SET A TRAP

HE'LL BE HERE ANY MINUTE

SOONER THAN YOU THINK, MY GUY

BUT IT WAS ROBIN WHO CAPTURED GUY

I'LL PAY A RANSOM IF YOU SET ME FREE!

YOU MEAN A SORT OF PENNY FOR THE GUY?

Shakespeare's Stratford

Most visitors to Stratford go there to see the place where William Shakespeare lived.

You can see the house where he was born in Henley Street. You can also see the spot where he lived after he became rich and famous – the house was called New Place and it stood opposite the Guild Chapel on Chapel Street.

Shakespeare bought it in 1597 and moved there when he retired in 1611.

But it's not there now.

The destruction of New Place is a tale of revenge and spite ... and tourists.

No more New Place

By the middle of the 1700s Shakespeare's plays were so popular people came from all over Europe to see the place where he had lived.

King James I wanted England to produce its own silk and so brought lots of mulberry trees to the country. Shakespeare was sent a mulberry cutting and he planted it in his garden. The terrible tourists would hop over the wall and pinch a twig or two from the famous tree.

Imagine living in that house – people peering in your windows, trampling over your garden and un-twigging your tree.

You'd have to be patient to put up with that.

In 1759 the Reverend Francis Gastrell lived at New House and he was not patient...

First he cut down the tree and left it as a pile of logs in the garden.

The people of Stratford were furious and they started to smash the potty priest's windows.

Then Gastrell was driven mad by orders for him to pay a £2 tax. That was when he took the most terrible revenge of all. He gathered a gang of servants and gave them the awful order…

The furious people of Stratford drove him out of the town. It is said that there is a ban on anyone called Gastrell ever living in Stratford again.

Did you know…?

A local watchmaker, Thomas Sharp, bought the mulberry logs and carved them into cups and boxes and toys for tourists. You know the sort of thing…

But he somehow managed to make enough toys for twenty trees! Maybe he cheated.

The house where Shakespeare's wife lived, Anne Hathaway's cottage, has survived. Shakespeare's daughter, Susanna, lived at Hall's Croft and you can still visit that. The house of Mary Arden, Shakespeare's mother, is also still there.

Even the mulberry tree at the flattened New Place is supposed to have grown from the chopped stump of Shakespeare's tree.

Magistrate not straight

Thomas Sharp wasn't the only Stratford man to make a dishonest living.

Justice Jones was a magistrate in Tudor times. He sat in court and heard the criminal cases.

But Justice Jones got greedy. He started to wander the Stratford taverns at night and chat to the criminals.

He would threaten them.

It was blackmail. At first the criminals paid up, but after a while they grew tired of Justice Jones's unjust threats.

One dark Stratford night he was murdered in the street.

There were four constables to keep the peace in sixteenth-century Stratford and one was called John Shakespeare – William Shakespeare's father. He was told to watch out for young men coming to Stratford for a good night out. These young troublemakers carried daggers and got into fights. John Shakespeare was told…

Did you know…?

In 1596 Shakespeare's son, Hamnet, died. He may have had the plague.

Beware of the sheep

A visitor to Stratford has to beware Sheep Street. To walk down there you have to be very brave or very foolish. It could be the most DANGEROUS street in the world! A street with an awful axeman, a deadly disease and a weird witch who was whacked.

We sent a researcher (who was brave AND stupid) to find out the facts behind the fantasies. She was armed only with a pen and a notebook.

Here are the terrifying tales…

The plague in Sheep Street

Stratford was a market town that bought and sold wool … and a lot of the wool came to 'Sheep Street', of course.

Thomas Gethin was a weaver who turned the wool into cloth and he lived at the Mercer's Building – it's now called the Garrick Inn. (A mercer was a cloth-dealer.)

Weaver Tom bought some wool from Europe and it came with some little extra passengers … fleas. As Tom might have said…

The fleas bit him and their bites carried bubonic plague. Tom felt ill and broke out in purple blotches. Within a couple of days he was dead.

Fleas do NOT like drinking cold blood … can you blame them? YOU wouldn't like drinking cold blood. So they hopped on to the nearest rat or human and bit them. Tom's poor wife Joanna was the next to go, nine days later.

That's how the plague spread from Sheep Street. In a few months about 250 Stratford people died horribly.

The axeman of Sheep Street

In the Middle Ages, John Davies used to travel the Midlands sharpening knives for people. But for himself he sharpened an axe. Davies attacked women and chopped them to pieces…

IT'S NOT AS IF HE AXED ME NICELY!

You may see his ghost in Sheep Street as an unshaven man in a white shirt and brown jacket. He has his axe in a leather bag.

If you don't see him then you may know he is there by the smell of his stinking breath.

The old witch of Sheep Street

Jane Ward was a poor and simple-minded old woman in 1867. But local people said, 'She's a witch, you know.'

Strange but true: ANOTHER John Davies lived in Sheep Street in those days… He was worried about his sick daughter. He got it into his head that old Jane was making her sick with witchcraft. Davies told a wild tale of magic…

He went to the police but they laughed at him, so Davies took the law into his own hands.

He waited in the shadows for Jane to return home one evening. As she walked down Sheep Street he jumped out with a knife and slashed her face.

Old Jane died a few days later. What happened to Davies?
a) He went free.
b) He was given six months in prison.
c) He was hanged with his knife around his neck.

Answer: b) He served just six months in prison – witch doesn't sound very fair on Jane.

The witch-child of Sheep Street

But Jane Ward was LUCKY! At least she lived to a good old age. Poor little Lucy died horribly a hundred years before Jane in the 1700s.

At number 40 Sheep Street is the Shrieve's House – named after William Shreyve who lived there in the 1530s. Shrieve House used to be a tavern and Lucy was the maid there. Her mother was said to be a witch. The woman refused to confess so the witch-finders turned on Lucy.

• First they tied her up.
• They burned her hands – Lucy said she knew nothing.
• They burned her feet – Lucy still said she knew nothing.
• In their fury they opened her belly and pulled out her guts – Lucy said nothing.

People who have their guts ripped out don't usually say a lot.

Lucy was only eight years old. Now she haunts the Shrieve's House and strokes the hair of visitors or plays with their jewellery.

She has been seen playing in an upstairs room – sometimes with her guts hanging out.

The spooksome Shrieve's House

Many people have lived and died in the Shrieve's House since the house was built in the mid-1250s.

But, for some reason, the people who died there seem to hang around as ghosts.

If you want to see/feel/smell a ghost then go there because it is said to be the most haunted house in England.

How many ghosts?
a) four
b) fourteen
c) forty

Answer: **c)** there have been reports of at least forty different ghosts. They include...

• William Shreyve, the friendly old owner who never misses a midnight ghost-watch in the barn at the back of the house.

• The strangled soldier from the 1600s. He got into a drunken fight one night. He was killed and buried in the barn.

• John Davies, the axeman of Sheep Street.

• And Lucy, the witch-child of Sheep Street.

The Shrieve's House is now a museum of Stratford history called 'The Falstaff Experience'.

Deadly drama

The Tudor age is famous for its theatre. Great writers like Shakespeare created plays which are performed all around the world to this day.

But where did Will get these great plays? Did William Shakespeare just sit down one day and say, 'I am going to write a great play'?

Of course not.

In the Middle Ages the workers in the towns had produced religious plays, often based on Bible stories. Travelling players often visited Stratford.

But they weren't just a way of preaching to people on stage. They were FUN...

• devils sprang from trapdoors
• god and his angels swooped down from cranes
• hell's mouth opened and belched out smoke
• floods, fires and earthquakes were staged
• characters suffered gory executions and wounds
• animals like rabbits and rams appeared for sacrifices
• costumes and masks were dazzling
• singing and dancing was loud and lively

They enjoyed the torturing of animals for sport. In the courtyards of inns there was cock-fighting, bear-baiting and bull-baiting.

In 1584 a foreign visitor to the London Beargarden described the cheerful little scene and the same sort of thing must have been seen in Stratford...

There is a round building three storeys high in which are kept about a hundred large English dogs, with separate wooden kennels for each for them. These dogs were made to fight one at a time with three bears, the second bear being larger than the first and the third larger than the second. After this a horse was brought in and chased by the dogs and, at the end, a bull who defended himself bravely.

The trouble is the bears needed a rest every other day. What could the bear-pit owners do to entertain the Elizabethans on the bear's day off? Give them those plays!

Don't give them the clever poetic plays of the students. Give them a bit of the glamour and guts of the old religious plays.

But Shakespeare couldn't give them the religion of those old plays, of course – doing religion could have got him hanged, burned and chopped in Tudor times!

Instead he went back to the Roman theatre. He took ideas from writers like Seneca, whose favourite subjects were crime and revenge, witches and ghosts, and they were very popular. The Romans loved tales of horror. Shakespeare probably read Seneca's gruesome plays at school.

William Shakespeare was a clever man. When he started writing at the end of the 1580s he was going to give the Beargarden mob the sort of fun they wanted ... he was going to give them horror.

Play dead

Go to Stratford today and you can see lots of murder and violence, torture and execution, suicides and cruelty.

The good news is it is all on stage and the blood is make-believe. Go to a Shakespeare play and there is a good chance you'll see some of the most horrible things ever to appear on a theatre stage.

For a start there are lots of interesting ways to be murdered.

Now you could probably think of a few ways to kill your characters in a play...

Stabbed, like Claudius in *Hamlet*...

IS THIS A DAGGER WHICH I SEE...ER... BEHIND ME?

Hanged like Cordelia in *King Lear*…

Killed in a battle like Sir Richard Ratcliffe in *Richard III*…

Strangled like Prince Humphrey in *Henry VI*…

Or even burned at the stake like Joan of Arc in *Henry VI*…

But Shakespeare liked to include unusual ways of killing people. If you wrote plays, how many of this top ten would you show?

1 Cut down in battle and head lopped off – Macbeth in *Macbeth*

2 Throat cut then baked into a pie and served to his mother – Chiron in *Titus Andronicus*

3 Assassinated by twenty-three men with daggers – Julius Caesar in *Julius Caesar*

4 Chased and eaten by a bear[2] – Antigonus in *The Winter's Tale*

5 Poison poured in the ear – King Hamlet in *Hamlet*

2 In Shakespeare's day a real bear was borrowed from the bear pit and sent on stage to chase the actor off.

6 Stabbed with a poisoned sword – Prince Hamlet in *Hamlet*

7 Smothered with a pillow – Desdemona in *Othello*

8 Stabbed and body thrown to wild beasts – Tamora in *Titus Andronicus*

9 Blown to pieces by a cannonball – Earl Salisbury in *Henry VI*

10 Buried chest-deep in the earth and left to starve to death – Aaron in *Titus Andronicus*

… and a few suicides…

1 Get a poisonous snake to bite you – Cleopatra in *Antony and Cleopatra*

2 Jump off a castle wall – Lady Macbeth in *Macbeth*

3 Throw yourself into a river (when you can't swim) – Ophelia in *Hamlet*

4 Drink poison – Romeo in *Romeo and Juliet*

5 Stab yourself – Juliet in *Romeo and Juliet*

6 Get a servant to hold a sword while you run on to it – Brutus in *Julius Caesar*

7 Swallow hot coals – Portia in *Julius Caesar*

8 Stab yourself with your friend's sword – Titinius in *Julius Caesar*

...and a bit of torture...

Lavinia (in *Titus Andronicus*) has her tongue cut out and her hands cut off to stop her speaking or writing the name of a villain.[3]

3 Don't worry, she uses the stumps of her wrists to grab a stick and write his name in the sand. He gets horribly got later in the play.

Did you know…?

In Stratford in the 1980s a theatre company performed Shakespeare's play *King Lear* with lots of realistic violence. In one scene the character called Gloucester has his eyes torn out. The stage manager made eyes out of a jelly substance; the actors pretended to tear them from the victim's eye sockets and throw them away.

On the first night the scene went beautifully – the audience gasped with horror. But on the second night the actors could hardly act. They were choking, trying to say the sad words yet bursting to laugh instead.

Why?

Because the jelly eyes had stuck to the scenery. The actors were trying to act seriously with a pair of jelly eyes staring at them!

The Royal Shakespeare Theatre

You may get more thrills here than just plays on the stage!

The Swan Theatre

Maybe the Swan Theatre is jealous of the Royal Shakespeare Theatre ghost so it has to have its own.

The Swan Theatre ghost is also a lady. She likes plays by the Russian writer Chekhov but she disappears if she doesn't like the performance.

The Swan ghost goes around slamming doors in the theatre but you know she has been there because she leaves behind a strong smell of perfume.

Orful Olimpicks

Most clever books will tell you the modern Olympic Games were first held in 1896 in Athens.

Those clever books forget that 'The Olimpicks' were held at Kingscombe Plain near Stratford in Shakespeare's day. (He may have been a bit old to take part but he could have gone to watch.)

A book of poetry was written about the games in 1636, but the games are likely to have started some time between 1601 and 1612.

Here are some Stratford games from Stuart times you may like to try...

Shocking for shins

Wrestling was a sport in these Olimpicks. You were allowed to hook your opponent's leg to bring him down. You were also allowed to kick his shins.

The shin-kicking was so popular that the crowds wanted to watch nothing else.

Shin-kicking became a sport. (These days some top football players are paid £50,000 a week to do it.)

Horrible Histories note: Shin-kicking is NOT allowed to be played by anyone under the age of 18. However, it is VERY suitable for two teachers to play. Draw a 2-m circle on the school yard, find two teachers and get them to try it today.

Shin-Kicking

This ancient sport is played by two people

YOU need:

A 2-METRE CIRCLE MARKED ON THE GRASS

A PAIR OF BOOTS FOR EACH PLAYER

To Play

① Throw a coin to decide who starts.

② Both contestants stand inside the circle.

③ The first contestant kicks his or her opponent on the shin. (Any contestant kicking the ankle or the knee will be banned).

BOOT!

④ The second contestant kicks the first contestant on the shin. The person taking the kick must not move the shin or they will lose.

WHACK!

⑤ The kickers take turns. They may kick the same shin each time or change shins.

⑥ The first kicker to step outside the circle is the loser.

HOP!

Hurling the hammers

Like in the modern Olympics, hammer-throwing was a popular sport, but back then they used REAL hammers (the modern sports hammer couldn't hit a nail if it tried).

Hammer-Throwing

This is a contest to see who can throw a hammer furthest.

You need: A sledgehammer and a line in the grass.

To play:

① Each contestant has three throws of the hammer.

Everyone must use the same hammer so there is no cheating using light hammers.

② You may whirl the hammer over your head but must not step over the line.

③ The hammer must go forward. If it slips out backwards and kills someone in the crowd then the throw will not be counted.

④ Any throw that hits a bird in flight will get a 5-metre bonus.

Horrible Histories tip: do not try this sport near a greenhouse.

There were also stick-throwing contests.

The really great thing about this sport is you don't need to go and get the stick after you've thrown it. Any dog will do it for you.

Clonking with cudgels

Sword-fighting skills were a matter of life or death in Stuart times.

To play:

1, The two contestants stand in the centre of the box and cross swords. The stickler (or referee) stands between them with a wooden rod.

2, The stickler raises his rod and knocks the swords apart.

3, The fighters fence for three minutes. If there is no winner then they take a one-minute break and carry on with another round.

WHUMP!

4, The winner is the first one to make his opponent's head bleed!

Wooden swords were used so that contestants wouldn't be killed, but a crack on the head was still painful.

Did you know…?
In Stuart times (1600s) gentlemen were using thin metal swords called rapiers. In Tudor times (1500s) they had used huge broadswords. In 1599 an old man called George Silver moaned that these new rapiers weren't so good as the old broadsword. He said...

> *A slashing blow from a broadsword puts the enemy's life in danger, it cuts through the veins, muscles, and sinews, and destroys the bones.*

Of course old George forgot to mention that your enemy might just chop you first and destroy YOUR bones.

Horrible Stratford quiz

How much do you know about the disgusting happenings in old Stratford? Here's a chance to find out. Score ten and you are a genius. Score eleven and you're a cheat.

1 Which of these was a common Stratford crime in the early 1500s?
a) Child-beating
b) Parent-beating
c) Teacher-beating

2 Thomas Harman was a judge. In 1566 he caught a beggar who refused to own up to his crime. What did Harman do to the beggar?
a) Had him locked up in prison anyway – unfair
b) Let the beggar go so he could catch him begging – sneaky
c) Tortured the beggar – cruel

3 In Tudor times what would you do to someone you argued with?
a) Spit at them
b) Punch them in the mouth
c) Write them a nasty letter

4 If you didn't catch the plague then Stratford could be a healthy place to live. After all, Francis Ange of Stratford, born in 1633, moved to America and lived a lot longer than most. He lived to what age?
a) 114 **b)** 124 **c)** 134

5 Nine miles south of Stratford is the village of Halford. There the villagers have a curious custom. On the eighth minute of the eighth hour of the eighth day of the eighth month each year they do what?

a) Throw cheese at an invisible rat
b) Eat cheese dressed as rats
c) Feed rats with poisoned cheese

6 Just up the Avon from Stratford is a place called Guy's Cliff. What did Lady Felice do at the cliff around AD 930?
a) Climbed the cliff to escape a kidnap gang
b) Jumped off the cliff because she was so unhappy
c) Slipped on the edge, got stuck halfway down and starved to death

7 In 1558 a Stratford councillor, Richard Symonds, was fined. What had he done?
a) Got drunk and punched the mayor on the nose
b) Let his ducks wander down the streets of Stratford
c) Parked his wagon on a double yellow line outside the town hall

8 What did 1560s Stratford butchers do with the heads and guts of the animals they killed?
a) Threw them in the street
b) Threw them in the river Avon
c) Ate them

9 In 1576 Stratford had a visit from an inspector to make sure they were not breaking a new law. Which law?
a) All women must walk backwards in front of their husbands on the way to church.

b) All dogs must be kept on a lead and their poop must be scooped off the Stratford streets.

c) All men must wear woollen caps to church on Sunday.

10 In 1600 the great doctor John Hall moved to Stratford and married Shakespeare's daughter, Susanna. He used herbs to cure people. But many Tudor doctors used what to cure warts?

a) A dead spider **b)** A dead horse **c)** A dead mouse

Answers:

1b) Yes, parents were battered by their children.

Other odd crimes reported at that time were…
* swearing by priests
* lending money
* playing dice
* opening a shop on Sunday.
  And, nicest of all…
* being sick in church!

2c) Judges were not supposed to torture prisoners but Harman didn't think there was much harm in it. (Harman … Harm-in it … geddit? Oh, never mind.)
Harman said…

> *The beggar refused to talk. I hung him up by the wrists until he did.*

Harman left him to hang for a few hours. Not a vicious torture but enough to make a weak old man give in.

A law passed in 1536 said that people caught outside their home town, without work, were to be punished by being whipped through the streets. If they were caught a second time they had part of an ear chopped off. If a homeless person was caught a third time he (or she) was hanged.

A law passed in 1597 didn't even give you an ear-clipping second chance. It said…

> *Every vagabond or beggar shall be stripped naked from the middle upwards and whipped in public until his or her body be bloody. He shall then be sent back to the town parish where he was born. If any vagabond or beggar return again, he shall suffer death by hanging.*

Horrible Harman said they deserved it...

> *They are punished by whippings. Yet they like this life so much that they soon forget. They do not think of changing until they climb the steps to gallows.*

...and then it is too late, of course.

3a) Spitting at someone showed how much you hated them. Of course men and women in the pillory would have people spitting on them. You would expect that.

But if a boy asked a girl to go out with him, and she didn't like him, then she would spit at him to show him how she felt!

Horrible Histories warning: Don't try this at school, girls. Even a priest who argued with another priest would often end up spitting. But that wasn't the worst thing that went on in Stratford churches. There were complaints that people went to church and...
• talked
• ate
• slept
• piddled
... during the service. (But not all at the same time.)

☠ THE HORRIBLE ☠ HIGHLIGHTS OF STRATFORD-UPON-AVON

❶ Shakespeare's Birthplace
Will was born here on 23 April 1564 – St George's Day. He died 52 years later on the same date – that must have really spoiled the birthday party.

❷ Town Hall
This used to be the Market Hall but then some rowdy Royalists decided to blow up their Civil War enemies, the Roundheads, so they packed the hall full of gunpowder… Find out the explosive results on pages 57-8.

❸ The Shrieve's House
In the middle of Stratford on busy Sheep Street is probably the most haunted house in England. Turn to pages 26-7 if you dare and find out about its spooky visitors – from the awful axe-man to the woeful witch child.

❹ Clopton Bridge
Sir Hugh Clopton had this bridge built over the Avon in 1490. No need to ford the river now. They should have changed the town's name to Strat-bridge. They didn't. Find out about some of the more miserable members of the Clopton family on pages 88-9.

❺ The Royal Shakespeare Theatre
The perfect spot to witness murder and violence, torture and execution, ghosts and witchcraft – all on stage, of course. Check out pages 30-5 and discover some of the horriblest moments from Shakespeare's plays.

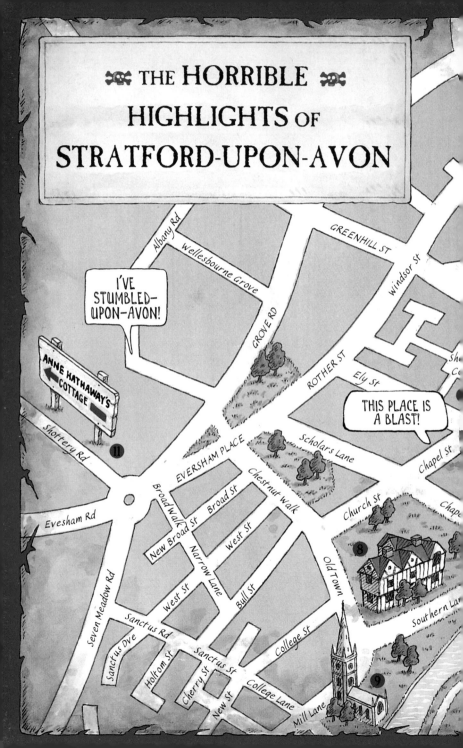

The Swan Theatre
Watch out where you sit in this theatre! You might be beside a ghostly critic... Find out more about Stratford's spectral spectators on page 37.

 New Place

Shakespeare retired to his home, New Place, in 1611 - but there's no trace of New Place now. The destruction of New Place is a tale of revenge and spite ... and tourists (see pages 18-19).

8 Hall's Croft
In 1600 the great doctor John Hall moved to Stratford and married Shakespeare's daughter, Susanna. You can drop in and check out some of the Doc's herbal remedies.

9 Holy Trinity Church
Will's buried here and he put a famous curse on anyone who tried to move his bones... But did someone steal Shakie's skull anyway? Turn to pages 91-2 and read the rotten rumours.

10 Mary Arden's House

For over 70 years tourists visited a place known as 'Mary Arden's House' to see where Will's mum had grown up ... but in November 2000 it was discovered that they'd been going to the wrong house! Now you can visit the real Mary Arden's House.

11 Anne Hathaway's Cottage
You can visit the house where Shakespeare's wife grew up – and see where the young Will went a-wooing.

4c) Young Francis remembered the execution of Charles I (when Francis was 16 years old). He then moved to Maryland, America, and ended his life in 1767 still with a good memory and married to his young wife who was only 80 years old.

5a) In AD 888 the peasants of Halford were starving. Rats were eating their crops. So at 8:08 on the eighth day of the eighth month in the year 888 they started to throw cheese down for the rats so they would stay away from the crops.

It worked!

Now, every year, the villagers do the same thing so the rats won't come back and attack the crops. They go in procession and throw the cheese into the river – for the rats that no one can see. They then perform a play about the rat legend. Go along one year and ask...

Horrible Histories note: Halford churchyard is haunted by a spook. If the rats don't get you then the ghosties and ghouls just might!

6b) The old story says Guy of Warwick fell in love with Felice. To win her hand he went off and killed a giant and the monstrous Dun Cow.

But then he felt sorry for his cruelty to cows and became a good Christian. He went to the Holy Land on a pilgrimage. When he came home he saved England from another giant – a Viking called Colibrand. (He chopped off the giant's arm and then his head.)

Guy came back to Guy's Cliff and lived in a cave as a hermit. At last Lady Felice found him, but Guy died in her arms. She was a bit upset so she threw herself off Guy's Cliff into the river Avon. The end.

BYE, GUY, MUST FLY!

A fine house was built at Guy's Cliff but it is ruined and haunted now.

7b) Richard was a top councillor, an alderman. He let his ducks and his pigs roam the streets of Stratford.

The streets were dangerous in Tudor times. If the pigs didn't get you then the dogs might – they were supposed to have muzzles fitted to stop them biting but owners forgot. If you were caught with a dangerous dog you could be fined.

They didn't have double yellow lines in those days, of course. Still, Stratford street-parking WAS a problem. Robert Rogers was a pest because he kept leaving his cart outside his front door in Sheep Street. He was fined. (Double yellow lines may not have been invented but it seems traffic wardens had!)

8a) In 1563 there was plague in London and people there blamed the rotting flesh in the streets. Stratford people started to get worried about the rotten guts that their butchers threw out of their shops.

The butchers' nasty customs were stopped. But in July 1564 the plague arrived anyway. Butchers weren't blamed. It was reported…

THE TOWN CLERK, RICHARD SYMONDS, HAS BEEN ACCUSED OF SPREADING THE DISEASE BY ALLOWING HIS SERVANT TO RUN AROUND THE TOWN WHILE HE WAS SICK WITH THE PLAGUE

So: Stratford servants spreading sad sickness, then.

9c) Queen Elizabeth got a lot of taxes from the wool dealers. So the more wool people used the richer Queen Liz got. In 1571 she had a new law passed. It said that all men had to wear woollen hats to church.

Not many people in Stratford knew about the law and not many wore the woollen caps.

Liz sent her inspectors around to check up. We don't know what happened but no one was convicted.

10c) You might like to try it for yourself.

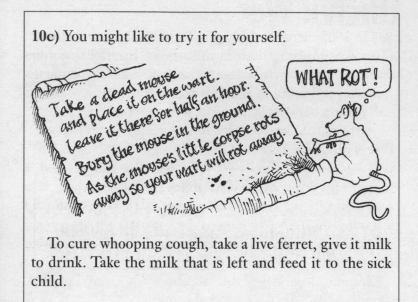

Take a dead mouse and place it on the wart. Leave it there for half an hour. Bury the mouse in the ground. As the mouse's little corpse rots away so your wart will rot away.

WHAT ROT!

To cure whooping cough, take a live ferret, give it milk to drink. Take the milk that is left and feed it to the sick child.

Uncivil War

In the 1640s, England was at war – with itself! Supporters of King Charles (Royalists) battled with Parliament's supporters (Roundheads). And some of the biggest battles took place around Stratford.

The evils of Edgehill

At 1:30 on 23 October 1642 a Royalist army faced a Roundhead army about ten miles from Stratford at a battlefield called Edgehill. King Charles I was in command of the Royalists.

The Royalists were in a hurry to start – they were running out of food! They marched down the hill.

Cannon fired and the Roundheads were blasted. Roundhead sergeant Henry Foster said...

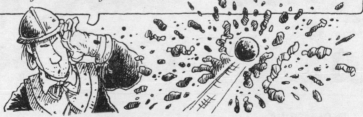

The enemy's cannon were somewhat dreadful when bowels and brains flew in our faces.

By the end of the day Charles claimed that he'd won – but so did Cromwell!

Charles's nephew, Prince Rupert, led a charge of horse soldiers. It was a great success. They broke through the Roundhead lines and reached the enemy supply wagons. But the nutty nephew didn't know what to do next.

His Cavaliers spent some time robbing the enemy supplies. Well, they had been short of food, remember.

At last they decided to join the battle again. Sadly they were too late. Charles was already running away to Oxford. He was sure they were losing.

Really it was a draw.

Bleeding bodies

When the battle of Edgehill was over and night fell then figures started to flit over the fields.

Were they going to bury the dead? Or help the groaning, moaning wounded?

No. They were going to rob the bodies; empty the pockets, strip the clothes.

It was a very chilly night. What if you were wounded and a thief tore off your clothes? The cold would kill you, wouldn't it?

THE ILL CHILL WILL KILL AT EDGEHILL!

WRONG!!!

Sir Gervase Scroop found that the freezing night stopped his wounds from bleeding. He had fallen with sixteen wounds and been left for dead.

His son found him two days after the battle and Sir Gervase lived. He lived another ten years in fact. The clothes thief saved his life.

I'D STILL LIKE ME BEST BOOTS BACK THOUGH!

Another gentleman called Bellingham was found by his friends after THREE days with TWENTY wounds. But the wounds turned bad with smelly gangrene and he died ten days later.

Wounds going rotten were a problem in those days. Colonel Sandys suffered more than most. A report said...

In his thigh the flesh rotted more each day and went bad. It was cut away a little at a time till it went down to the bare bone. It stank so badly he could not bear the smell and nor could his friends. He spent one month ranting in pain and then Colonel Sandys died. His son visited him, caught smallpox and also died.

Not every story had an unhappy ending.

Sir Hugh Ackland was taken home to Devon after the battle. He got a fever and then went cold and stiff.

He was put in his coffin and a drunken servant was left to watch over him. The servant knew Sir Hugh had liked a drink when he was alive. He said…

Master loved brandy dearly when he was alive, and now, though he is dead, I am sure he shall have a glass with us!

He poured some brandy into the mouth of the corpse.

Sir Hugh coughed and spluttered. He lived … and when he died many years later he left that drunken servant a lot of money in his will.

Phantoms of the phight

Two months after the battle some farm workers near Edgehill complained that they were disturbed at night by the charging of horses, the roar of cannon and the blowing of bugles. The villagers went to see what was happening … and they saw the battle of Edgehill – again.

And again.

And again … and again. Ghosts seemed to be acting out the battle every weekend.

Charles sent some of his officers to report and they saw the battle too. Charles's reporters had been there for the original battle and recognised some of the ghostly soldiers. They saw Sir Edmund Verney who had been holding the king's flag until his hand was cut off - still holding the flagpole.

The ghostly battle can still be seen every year on 23 October, it is said. They also pop up a week later around Halloween.

Brook case

In 1643 the Royalists had been driven out of Stratford.

The new Roundhead general in charge of Stratford was Lord Brooke. He was popular and his men loved him, but he was hated by the Royalists in Stratford.

In February Brooke told his captains to meet him in the Market Hall in Sheep Street.

Meanwhile, the Royalists planted five barrels of gunpowder in the cellars and planned to blow the Roundheads into little pieces – little but rather sticky pieces.

They lit the fuse and ran for cover.

But…

Lord Brooke was nowhere near the Market Hall at the time.

No one was hurt. But the Market Hall was wrecked.[4]

No one remembers this great event! School children in Stratford, to this very day, do not sing …

REMEMBER, REMEMBER, FEBRUARY 1643 GUNPOWDER, TREASON AND A PLOT GONE TO POT!

But Royalist readers will be pleased to know Lord B didn't last much longer. He left Stratford later that month to attack Lichfield. A Royalist with a musket hid in the tower of Lichfield Cathedral and shot Brooke in the head.

4 It's the Town Hall now. If you go there just make sure you don't drop any lighted matches.

The strung-up spy

In 1651 another Civil War battle was fought at Worcester, 25 miles from Stratford. It was the last battle and Charles II was in charge.

Just before the battle one of the Royalist spies was captured and taken to Stratford. He was questioned...

Hard times

Some things never change. Some of the horrible history stories of Stratford could still happen today.

Look at these stories and score them ✖ to ✖ ✖ ✖ ✖ ✖. That is ✖ if you think it wouldn't happen today or ✖ ✖ ✖ ✖ ✖ if you think it still does!

One of the spookiest tales happened on a bitterly cold night in Stratford on Thursday 13 January 1820…

Riding With the Dead

Ah but it was cold that night. The wind swept through the icy Stratford streets from the north-east. In Barton Street the thermometer said it was 18 degrees below freezing – that is minus 10 in celsius.

A horse-drawn wagon clattered down the cobbles and turned into the tavern. 'We're there!' the driver said to his passenger. But there was no reply.

The driver jumped down and shrugged. 'I'll let you sleep then, you poor old beggar.' He put his horse in the stable and fed it, then went inside to a blazing log fire and a mug of hot ale.

It was 10 p.m. when he went out to check on the horse. 'It's warmer inside!' he called to his passenger. 'The landlord's a good man. He won't charge you to sleep by the fire tonight.'

He shook the old man gently. He was as cold and stiff as the ice crust on the Sheep Street trough. 'God rest your soul,' the driver murmured and went back inside.

The next day the magistrate heard the story of the dead man – William Stringer. Not a story of a gentle end to a miserable life. But a story of human cruelty … such cruelty it was almost murder.

Old William had been walking to Birmingham when he fell ill at Enstone near Oxford. He was taken to the local workhouse to recover.

The overseer was a man called John Russell – a man with flint where his heart should have been. After a few days he said, 'You don't belong here, Stringer. You're well enough to travel. Get out.'

'Another week, sir. Another week till I'm stronger, please. One more week?' old William whined.

Russell jabbed at him with a bony finger. 'You will go today if I have to carry you out on my own back. There's a wagon leaving for Birmingham now. You will be on it. The good people of Enstone aren't paying to keep you another day. No, not another hour. Not another minute!'

He dragged the old man to his feet and out of the door. He hauled him on to the wagon. 'You'll not need food. You'll be in Stratford by nightfall. Let them feed you.'

A woman was passing and gave old William a bottle of gin and a piece of pudding. 'To warm you on the journey,' she said.

The old man smiled weakly. He was too weak to eat. But the little kindness warmed him. He was probably dead before the wagon reached Stratford.

The magistrate raged against the workhouse-keeper of Enstone. 'William Stringer died of natural causes … but he would still be alive today if John Russell had done his duty. John Russell is not just a disgrace to Enstone – he brings shame on the whole human race.'

An old person turned away by the people who are supposed to help him. An old person left to die alone and cold.

Could it happen today? ✺ ✺ ✺ ✺

Death of a pauper

William Shakespeare went from Stratford to London to make his fortune. Two hundred years later people were still making the same trip. But they were not all a success.

In July 1840 a newspaper reported this terrible case.

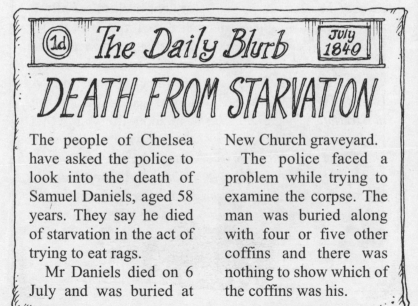

The Daily Blurb 1d July 1840

DEATH FROM STARVATION

The people of Chelsea have asked the police to look into the death of Samuel Daniels, aged 58 years. They say he died of starvation in the act of trying to eat rags.

Mr Daniels died on 6 July and was buried at New Church graveyard.

The police faced a problem while trying to examine the corpse. The man was buried along with four or five other coffins and there was nothing to show which of the coffins was his.

Mr Daniels came from Stratford-upon-Avon where he had kept the Three Tuns Inn. Mrs Daniels said they had arrived in London and gone to the workhouse. But there was not enough food to keep them alive. They moved to Paradise Row where they begged from people no richer than themselves. They lived a half-starved life, sleeping on straw and covered in rags.

FROM RAGS TO... MORE RAGS

Mrs Daniels did not ask for help from the council. She was told that she would be sent to work on the treadmill if she did.[5] Her husband fell ill and she went to the doctor. He said the man needed food, not medicine, and gave them nothing.

When her husband died she asked the council for a coffin but was refused at first. She was told she would be sent to prison or sent back to Stratford. She offered to throw herself into the river and save the council the trouble of burying her too. A coffin was granted at last and soon afterwards Mrs Daniels went to live with her nephew.

Mr and Mrs Daniels had tried to return to Stratford when Mr Daniels was ill but found it was worse than London.

5 The Treadmill was a huge hamster-wheel for humans where you walked for hours and went nowhere.

The book *Oliver Twist* describes the terrible Victorian workhouses in London. Mrs Daniels said pretty much the same about Stratford…

> *In the Stratford workhouse we were supposed to have porridge in the morning but were given boiled flour. The soup at dinner was very weak. My husband had a bag hung round his neck and was told to pick stones from the garden. He was very weak and could not stand it for more than two weeks. We complained but were told we could stay in or get out. If we left we would not be given even a crust of bread. It took us four days to walk back to London and that left him very weak.*

The choice in the Stratford workhouse was a horrible one.
 Do backbreaking work and get a little foul food OR
 Leave the workhouse and starve OR
 Beg and die chewing rags.
 Would it happen today? ✼

Death of a fox-hunter

Fox-hunting was a popular sport in England until it was banned in 2005. But in the Stratford area it wasn't always the fox that ended up dead!

On Friday 16 December 1842 *The Times* newspaper had this chilling report…

2d **THE TIMES** December 1842

DREADFUL DEATH

It is our sad duty to report another of those fearful events that are becoming too common in England. We mean the use of a knife in a quarrel leading to the death of one young man and the arrest of six others.

The scene of the tragedy was on the road from Worcester to Stratford. There are woods in that area, full of foxes, which are a nuisance to the farmers. These foxes are hunted by villagers with packs of hounds. When a fox is killed then it is taken to the nearest farmhouse and the farmer gives a reward.

On Saturday last, George Green, Edward Archer and six others caught a fox near Rous Lench and took it to the Bell Inn where they were rewarded with beer. When they left the inn, Green and Archer fell into a quarrel and began to fight.

While they were struggling Green suddenly cried out, 'I am stabbed!' He fell to the ground and almost instantly died.

Superintendent Harris of Pershore was called and Archer was arrested. No weapon was found on him. A search was made of the area though it was thick with tangled bushes and ditches. The hedges were cut down and the ditches drained and on Sunday morning the searchers were rewarded. A knife was found at the bottom of a drained ditch. Edward Archer has been charged with the murder.

A gang of young men get drunk. They fight. One pulls a knife and stabs another.

Would it happen today? ✂ ✂ ✂ ✂ ✂

You bet it would.

Railway riot

Stratford was quite a quiet place in the middle of England. Then, in July 1851, the railways arrived.

There was a train-load of trouble when the builders arrived to dig the tunnel at Mickleton, just south of Stratford.

The workers were called 'navvies' and they were the toughest labourers in the land – a bit like cowboys in the Wild West. And, like cowboys, they had their own battles with rival gangs.

The trouble at Mickleton began when the Marchant gang were sacked and the Betts gang moved in to take over.

The Times newspaper reported that the Marchants weren't going to give up their work without a fight. They were owed money. They even had the police on their side.

Each side gathered a small army of about 2,000 men…

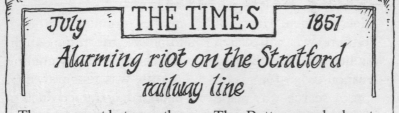

Alarming riot on the Stratford railway line

The argument between the workers from Marchant and the workers from Betts has reached a new and horrifying level.

The Betts company were allowed to raise a gang of 500 men and start work on the tunnel. But Mr Marchant was standing at the end of the bridge and dared any one of them to cross. He was well armed with pistols.

The Betts gang made a rush for the bridge but were driven back by Marchant's men. Several heads were cracked and three shoulders dislocated.

The Betts men had not, so far, used their pickaxe handles and shovels to fight. Now they grabbed a Marchant man who held a pistol and they almost smashed his skull in two.

There was a break in the fighting while the leaders talked. But in that time navvies began to fight once again. One man had a serious wound to the head while another had his finger bitten off.

It has now been agreed that work will stop for a fortnight.

This was the last battle fought by private armies in Britain.

But two gangs fighting with pickaxe handles and guns; fingers bitten off…

Would it happen today? ✶ ✶ ✶ ✶

Scary Stratford

Stratford and the country round it look peaceful enough. But don't be surprised if you meet some blood-chilling sights.

The Shakespeare Hotel

You may not always get a good night's sleep at The Shakespeare Hotel in Chapel Street. Not if you are disturbed by the ghostly cries of a girl.

It is said that an owner in the 1600s locked his daughter up there and never let her go out.

In time she starved to death and her hungry ghost haunts an upper room.

Ettington Park

Seven miles south of Stratford is a house called Ettington Park house, which belongs to the Shirley family. It has stood there since before Norman times. If you want to see, hear or feel a ghost then go there.

Ilmington

Ilmington village is about nine miles south of Stratford. In the 1700s, a huntsman went out with a pack of hounds. After a long day with nothing to eat the hounds went wild.

Shuckburgh Hall

Fifteen miles west of Stratford is Shuckburgh Hall.

Lieutenant Sharp of the army fell in love with the daughter of the Shuckburgh family but was told he couldn't see her again. He took one last walk with her in the garden of the house. He pulled out a pistol and shot her – then blew out his own brains.[6]

The ghostly couple are said to float through the flowers.

Atherstone on Stour

Three miles south of Stratford is the village of Atherstone on Stour. Watch out as you drive along the A34 road there. A ghostly walker crosses the road and vanishes through a brick wall.

6 It's surprising he had any to blow out. This was not a very clever thing to do. Anyone with half a brain cell would have shot the FATHER!! Do NOT try it in your own garden – it will make a mess on the lawn.

It's the ghost of a farmer. The man had a bet about how fast he could ride his horse in the dark. He set off at full speed to win his bet.

But he was hit by the branch of a tree, fell off and died.

Hilborough Manor

Seven miles west of Stratford is Hilborough Manor near Bidford. This is haunted by TWO ghosts from Tudor times.

The Warwickshire witches

Stratford through the ages has been awash with witchcraft. Here are just two of the strange tales from the area. Both are unsolved murders with a witchcraft mystery…

The Campden Wonder

Campden is just 10 miles south of Stratford. In 1660 a gruesome tale of murder and witchcraft was reported … it came to be known as The Campden Wonder.

On 16 August that year, old William Harrison set off to collect rents for Viscountess Campden. His pockets would have been full of money by the end of the day. He did not return that night.

The Viscountess sent out a servant, John Perry, to look for him. Perry came back next morning and said…

I FOUND HIS BLOODSTAINED HAT… IT'S BEEN SLASHED!

The law officers asked Perry questions and in the end he said…

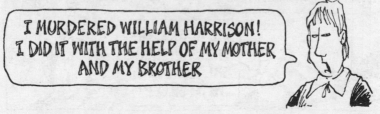

I MURDERED WILLIAM HARRISON! I DID IT WITH THE HELP OF MY MOTHER AND MY BROTHER

The body was not found, but Perry, his mother and brother went to trial. They were found guilty and hanged, all three on the same gallows.

Now here is the first creepy thing.

Perry was hanged in chains on the gallows and left to rot. His mother and brother were buried underneath the gallows in an open grave.

Three days after the execution a strange, well-dressed lady rode up to the gallows with a servant. She said...

No one knows why the lady wanted to see the body, but the corpse of a hanged person is supposed to have magic powers. But this corpse had a shocking power ... the power to scare the lady's horse.

The horse shot under the gallows where John Perry was swinging in chains. Perry's dead legs caught the lady on the head...

…and sent her flying. Where did she land?

In the open grave.

The would-be witch rode off and was never seen again. But THAT'S not the Campden Wonder. The Campden Wonder came two years later.

William Harrison turned up in Campden. Yes, Harrison the 'murdered' man. He said…

I WAS ATTACKED BY THREE STRANGERS, TAKEN ON TO A SHIP AND SOLD AS A SLAVE IN TURKEY. I ESCAPED AND CAME HOME. HERE I AM

But Harrison was 70 when he was kidnapped. Why would anyone kidnap a 70-year-old for a slave? It's mystery number one.

Maybe Harrison just ran off with the rent money. He came back when it was spent and told the slave story?

And mystery number two … why did John Perry say he killed Harrison with the help of his mother and brother? He was probably mad. It got them all hanged.

And mystery number three: who was the strange witch lady who landed on the corpse of Mrs Perry?

We will never know.

Murder on Meon Hill

Just six miles to the south of Stratford are the Quinton villages and the flat-topped Meon Hill. It was the sort of place where ancient Druids might have made human sacrifices.

How did the hill get there? Charles Walton, a ploughboy, had heard the ancient story...

The Devil had left his mark and the area became known for its ghosts and witches.

A local vicar wrote a book about the area and it told a terrible tale...

> In 1875 a weak-minded young man had killed a woman named Ann Turner. He had killed her using a pitchfork because he believed she had bewitched him.

The killer had pinned the 'witch' to the ground with a pitchfork through the throat. When John Hayward was arrested he said he had to kill her to save the people from the witch. The pitchfork in the throat was to stop her rising from the dead. Hayward was hanged.

Ten years later young Charles Walton was living in the village of Lower Quinton and working near Meon Hill. As he walked home one night he met a phantom black dog.

He met it again the next night.

On the third night he met the dog but this time it was followed by a headless woman.[7]

The following day young Charles's sister died.

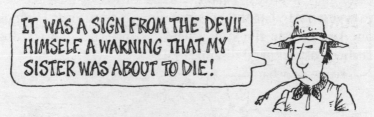

> IT WAS A SIGN FROM THE DEVIL HIMSELF. A WARNING THAT MY SISTER WAS ABOUT TO DIE!

Charles Walton became interested in witchcraft after that. His hobby was breeding toads. It was said he had a spell that would ruin a farmer's crops...

7 Maybe it was a guide dog! After all, if you're a headless woman you'd need one wouldn't you?

In 1945 Walton was 74 years old. One day he went out to work in the fields but was never seen alive again.

His body was found in a field ... with a pitchfork through his throat!

A blood sacrifice? Or an avenging farmer killing a witch to stop his toady attacks?

We'll never know because the police never solved the case. The detective in charge worked for weeks, then decided to give up. He left the police station in Stratford. He took one last walk in the killing field ... and a large black dog rushed past him and disappeared.

Creepy, or what?

Terrific toilets

Poor young Will Shakespeare. He must have woken up on many a cold night and wondered – should he go down the freezing garden to the toilet shed – the 'jakes' – or should he stay in bed?

What a decision. As he may have said to himself…

TO PEE, OR NOT TO PEE, THAT IS THE QUESTION

But did Shakespeare guess that a famous toilet factory would arrive in Stratford in 1998?

It is the Thomas Crapper factory. Visitors to Stratford can now enjoy historical Shakespeare plays AND historical toilets. Fascinate your friends with these terrific toilet tales …

1 Splashes and ashes

In Shakespeare's Stratford most people didn't have a room for the toilet. They usually had a 'chamber pot' – like a big cup with a handle. Shakespeare called this…

THE JORDAN!

One disgusting Tudor habit was to empty this potty into the ashes in the fireplace.

Even MORE disgusting people didn't even bother to do that – they just piddled straight into the fireplace.

2 Poo pits

You were supposed to collect your toilet waste and take it to a town 'cesspit'. Farmers could then collect it and spread the poo over their fields to help the grass grow.

But many people just tipped it into the rubbish dump at the end of the street.

The name Shakespeare would have used for the rubbish dump was...

THE MUCKHILL!

In Tudor Stratford people were fined for letting these stinking heaps grow too big, but they still did it.

A report of 1558 complained...

There are perfectly good muck heaps at the bottom of Bridge street, Sheep street, and the top of Scholars lane and Greenhill street, yet people will keep making dunghills all over town!

3 Jake in the box

Posher people had a shed in the garden for their toilet.

Inside there was a seat with a hole in it. The waste dropped through the hole and into a cesspit or a stream. (Further down the stream people could be drinking the water that you had just had a poo in – that's why there was so much disease in Tudor times.)

The name Shakespeare would have used for the toilet shed was…

THE HOUSE IN OFFICE OR THE JAKES!

4 Stool pool

In really, REALLY posh houses and castles you could have a room INSIDE the building for your toilet. In the toilet room there would be a chair. Lift the seat of the chair and there's a chamber pot underneath.

When you've finished you put the lid down to keep the worst of the smell out of the room. Shakespeare would have called these rooms…

THE STOOL ROOM OR THE PRIVY. IN A CASTLE IT WOULD BE CALLED THE GARDEROBE

5 Lizzie's loos

Queen Elizabeth travelled a lot around England. Why? Because she loved to see her people? No. Because of the toilets.

• Those old jakes emptied into a toilet pit.

• The toilets soon filled up when Elizabeth arrived with all her servants. After a few weeks in a house the stench would be terrible.

• All the Queen could do was move to another house. Soon that would be filled with the awful smell of the reeking jakes and she would move on again. Nowhere stays sweet-smelling for long.

• It didn't matter how much servants scrubbed and washed, how many times the jakes were emptied or how deep the pits that held the waste, the stink was always there.

• At Hampton Court the waste was emptied into drains that ran into the river Thames. Yet the drains smelt dreadfully in summer, which is why the Queen moved off to the fresh air of the country.

• Elizabeth travelled everywhere with her own toilet stool with a hinged lid. She would lift the lid so she could pee into the pot below then put the lid back down.

NONE OF HER LADIES-IN-WAITING ENJOY THE JOB OF EMPTYING THE POT BUT SOMEONE HAS TO DO IT OTHERWISE THE LIDDED STOOL BEGINS TO STINK THE ROOM OUT!

Mind you, this is not so foul as the servants who didn't bother with lidded stools. They simply used the palace courtyard.

Did you know...?
What did the Elizabethans use instead of toilet paper? A damp rag. It could be rinsed and used over again. (Oh, stop pulling a disgusted face. It was probably better than the hard toilet paper your mum and dad used to use!)

In really nasty Tudor prisons you weren't even given a cloth. And you thought school detention was bad?

6 Horrible Harrington

Will Shakespeare may have seen (but not tried) Britain's first flushing toilet.

The Queen's godson, Sir John Harrington, was sent from court in disgrace – he told rude stories to her ladies-in-waiting.[8]

He decided that to wheedle his way back into Elizabeth's affections what he needed was to build her a jakes that was so clean it would be a wonder to her eyes and to her fine nose. So he built a new type of toilet into his house. There is a tank of water above the toilet. The user sits on the seat and pees (or whatever) into fresh water. The user then pulls a handle on the seat and fresh water rushes down from the tank and flushes out the dirty water.

8 Elizabeth was called by creepy courtiers 'The Faerie Queene'. If Sir John was her godson then he's one of few men in England to have a real fairy godmother.

The dirty water is then sent into a large underground pit. There is still a problem of a smell rising from the pit and the thing will have to be emptied every year.

I CALL MY INVENTION THE AJAX... BECAUSE I HAVE BUILT 'A JAKES!'

No, not a great joke, but it is 400 years old and you won't sound too great when you're 400 years old.

The Queen saw the invention, ordered one for her own palace – and forgave her godson.

Shakespeare may have seen it when he visited her palace to perform a play for her Maj.

But Sir John's invention never became popular in his lifetime. People laughed at him and he never built another one.

The flushing toilet was a brilliant invention but it needed a good drainage system with proper sewers to make it really clean and healthy.

7 Cool Crapper

The terrible Tudor toilets began to change 300 years later when Thomas Crapper began to make good, cheap flushing toilets in the 1880s.

His salesmen travelled round Britain with little model toilets in their cases.

His shop in London had toilets in the windows. It is said that some Victorian ladies were so shocked they looked at them and fainted.

Thomas sold his toilets to kings and queens. He was the most famous toilet maker EVER.

8 Super for Stratford

Thomas died and had no children to carry on the toilet business. The NAME of the toilet company went on until 1966 and was then sold off.

You couldn't buy a Crapper toilet any longer. But in 1998 the old Thomas Crapper Company was bought by a new owner who had a passion for … er, bathrooms.

9 He did. In his play *Romeo and Juliet*. But at least Juliet has taken poison when she said it – she hadn't just been shocked at the sight of a toilet.

He started making Crapper toilets again. Where did he build his new shop?

In Stratford-upon-Avon, of course.

As Shakespeare almost said…

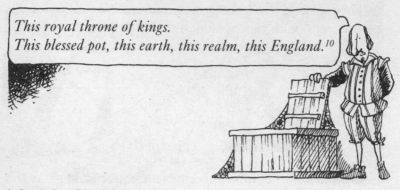

This royal throne of kings.
This blessed pot, this earth, this realm, this England.[10]

9 Sad for Shakespeare

What a pity Will Shakespeare never got to enjoy Thomas Crapper's terrific toilets.

But I am sure he dreamed of Crapper's toilet in his Stratford home. THAT'S why he wrote those famous lines in his play *Othello*…

Here is my journey's end, here is my butt.[11]

10 Yes, all right, Shakespeare said, 'this blessed PLOT', but really he should have said 'pot'.
11 Oh, very well, when he said 'butt' he meant the target where you practised your archery. 'Here is my butt' means I have reached my target. But butt has other meanings…

Cheerless church

Holy Trinity Church in Stratford has more visitors than any other parish church in England.

They go to see Shakespeare's grave. They can't see his corpse ... though they would probably like to.

Even a peaceful church like this has seen its share of horrible history.

Plague pain

Charlotte Clopton was the daughter of the richest family in Stratford but all her money couldn't save her. In 1564 Charlotte caught the plague. The Cloptons cried. They took Charlotte to Holy Trinity Church in Stratford and they buried her quickly, before anyone else caught the plague from her.

Too quickly.

They placed her body in a stone cellar under the church floor and went home to cry a little more.

Another Clopton died soon after and they opened up the cellar once again. But Charlotte's body had moved! She was leaning against the wall now. It seemed she had been buried alive, woken up and struggled to get free before dying a second time – from hunger and thirst.

The horrified mourners looked at her body and saw what had happened in her final struggle for food...

GOOD GOD! SHE HAS BITTEN A LUMP FROM HER OWN LEFT ARM!

Horrible Histories warning: There is no proof that this is a true story. In fact, the name 'Charlotte' was not used in England till a hundred years after Charlotte Clopton died.

The broken-hearted bride

One of Stratford's oldest houses is Clopton House – just over a mile north of Stratford, yes, the same one where Charlotte came to a miserable end in 1564.

About 30 years later Margaret Clopton was planning to get married, but her boyfriend went off and left her.

Miserable Margaret was so upset she threw herself down the well at the back of the house. You can see the well – just don't drink the water if there are bits of Margaret still in it. The sad story gave William Shakespeare the idea for a scene in one of his plays, *Hamlet*. A deserted girl, Ophelia, throws herself into a river.

Did you know...?

Margaret's sister was kidnapped by criminals and thrown off Clopton Bridge when her family didn't pay the ransom money.

Putrid plague

In 1645 Stratford suffered one of its worst attacks of the plague. The town council came up with a couple of ideas to stop it spreading. First they said…

BAD idea. Many of the wardens caught the plague. And, of course, when they left a plague house they often carried the disease wherever they went.

So the council came up with a new idea…

Would YOU go to a death village?

Stratford victims didn't want to die alone and be buried in a pit with dozens of other victims. So they went to Holy Trinity Church and sat on 'The Plague Wall'.

A plant with poisonous berries called deadly nightshade grew there. The victims ate the berries and fell off the wall into the churchyard. It was holy ground. They believed they had a better chance of going to heaven if they died that way.

Did you know…?

There were many rare plants growing in the shelter of the churchyard in the Middle Ages.

Stratford witches would go there to pick them and make their herbal medicines.

But many of their spells needed soil from a grave.

And if the witch wanted to make a spell to fly then they needed the fat from a dead child.

If you were buried in Holy Trinity Church you didn't always get to rest in peace.

The curious case of Shakespeare's skull

When Holy Trinity Church became too full the old skeletons would be dug up and the bones tumbled into a building near the church called a 'charnel' house.

William Shakespeare probably got at least one creepy story from the charnel house at Holy Trinity Church. In *Romeo and Juliet* the girl Juliet decides to fake her own death so she doesn't have to marry the awful young man Paris. She takes a drug to send her into a sleep like death. Juliet cries…

She talks about the stinking shinbones and the skulls with no jaws. Shakespeare probably saw these for himself.

He must have hated it, because when he was buried at Holy Trinity Church he had a verse already written for his tomb telling people NOT to dig him up and throw him in the charnel house!

12 You can see Shakespeare's curse today – just don't go digging up his bones!

There is a story that one man ignored the curse. In 1794 there was a party at Ragley Hall, eight miles west of Stratford. The drunken diners told an odd story...

I HAVE HEARD SIR HORACE WALPOLE HAS OFFERED A REWARD OF 300 POUNDS FOR THE SKULL OF SHAKESPEARE

Dr Frank Chambers of Alcester decided he would claim that reward. He hired three local men to raid the tomb and paid them three pounds each – that still left the disgusting doctor £291, didn't it?

It is said the men got the skull. But Walpole refused to pay the reward and told Dr Chambers to put it back.

The skull thieves failed to shift the gravestone the second time and they just hid the skull somewhere else. All Chambers had was a piece of bone that he'd chipped out. Fifty years later a spare skull was found sixteen miles from Stratford at Beoley Church. The chip of bone fitted perfectly.

Shakespeare's skull had been found! It was taken back to Stratford and buried with the body again.

Horrible Histories warning: There are lists of doctors in Alcester. There is no Dr Frank Chambers on the list. Did he ever exist? Is the whole story just a fairy tale? You'll have to dig up Shakespeare's corpse again and see if there is the famous chip in the skull!

Epilogue

Stratford-upon-Avon is famous all around the world for just one man who was born there – William Shakespeare, known as the Bard of Avon.

People go to Stratford just to see the place where he lived, and the place he died at the age of 52.

It is no surprise William Shakespeare died quite young because Tudor Stratford was a filthy, smelly and unhealthy place to live.

In 1594 William Lambarde made a speech about poverty in England. He was worried that soldiers were adding to the problem.

There were always poor lepers, poor old people, poor sick people, poor widows, poor orphans, and such like. There are also poor soldiers we rarely heard of till now. They live their lives in begging and we end them by hanging. They fight our wars and suffer cold and hunger while we live in comfort. They lie in the open field when we lie in our beds.

In August 2005 there was a report that said...

And, of course, it is ... today.

But Stratford has its own horrible history of pongy plagues and dreadful deaths.

Visit it today and you won't see much of the horrible history ... unless you meet one of the many Stratford ghosts, of course!

You might look at Stratford and say...

But if you meet Shakespeare's ghost he may say...

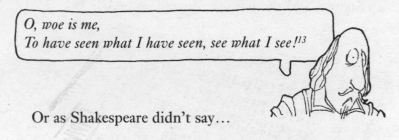

O, woe is me,
To have seen what I have seen, see what I see![13]

Or as Shakespeare didn't say…

THE PRESENT IS PLEASANT

But history can be HORRIBLE!

---

13 He wrote that in his famous play *Hamlet*.